WHAT'S
GOING ON
Lord?

POEMS OF FAITH BY
RICHARD CULLEN

VOLUME ONE

Mereo Books

1A The Wool Market Dyer Street Cirencester Gloucestershire GL7 2PR
An imprint of Memoirs Books Ltd. www.mereobooks.com

What's going on Lord?

ISBN: 978-1-86151-920-7

First published in Great Britain in 2019
by Mereo Books, an imprint of Memoirs Books Ltd.

Copyright ©2019

The address for Memoirs Books Ltd. can be
found at www.mereobooks.com

Memoirs Books Ltd. Reg. No. 7834348

Typeset in 11/15pt Century Schoolbook
by Wiltshire Associates Ltd.
Printed and bound in Great Britain by Biddles Books

Contents

Foreword, by Thomas M Burns SM

Acknowledgements

Introduction

What's Going On, Lord?	1	Dying Before Death	50
Turn to the Lord	3	Trinity/Priesthood	51
Unlock Your Heart	5	God's Gaze	53
Melt Into Your Presence	5	Dying to Self	55
True Friendships	7	Live in the Present	56
Loneliness	9	Silence, That Is YOU	57
Depression	11	A Merry Dance	59
His Greatest Story Ever Told	13	Eternity in Time	61
What Is Eternity?	15	The Spirit's Classroom	62
Healing Love	17	Deep Waves of Cleansing Sighs	63
Hope	19	Come Be With Me	65
Christmas Night	21	Strength Through Weakness	67
Time	24	Friendship	68
The Transfiguration	27	The Spoken Word of Silence	69
Presence Through Quietness	28	Saints	71
The Ego	29	The Spiritual Life	73
The Cell (Before the Crucifixion)	32	Who Is Christmas For?	77
Why, Jesus?	35	Hope Found After Suicide (for a young person)	78
The Eviction	36		
More, Never Less	39	Resurrection Message	79
Jesus to You	40	Here In Your Pain	81
Without You	41	Let Them Go	85
Why You Came	44	Thank You, Mum	86
Mary (The Annunciation)	45	That Nowhere Place	87
Heaven Is Within You	47		
Baptism	49		

Foreword

The poems in this book came home to me immediately as striking chords, clarifying situations that I am familiar with, putting into perspective things that had puzzled me, reflecting personal and relevant daily experiences of my own. Thanks to these punchy lines of poetry, I can now truly say:

THAT'S ME!

I'VE BEEN THERE!

I'M JUST LIKE THAT!

I KNOW WHAT YOU MEAN!

THAT MAKES A DIFFERENCE!

SO THAT'S WHAT IT WAS ALL ABOUT!

So, read on. Ponder and pause. When something lights up your mind and your heart, reflect for a moment. When the Spirit prompts you, dig into your memory for further insights. You won't be disappointed

+ Thomas Matthew

Tom M Burns SM

Bishop of Menevia

Acknowledgements

To Mary and Richard, my parents, who were the first to introduce me to Faith.

To my brother priests Fr. Gerald (deceased); Fr. Hugh for his appreciation of my poems; and Fr. Anthony, who having read and appreciated my poems insisted that they 'should be out there'. Without his invaluable input and practical support these poems would still be gathering dust.

To my sister, Sr. Agnes, who first introduced me to the Carmelite spirituality, which has been very formative in my spiritual development.

To my wonderful wife Diane, who was my sounding board and patient listener to my witterings as I tried to make sense of my poems.

To all my family, who through their prayers and support over the years have been a wonderful influence over my lifetime.

Photographs on pp 2, 8, 21, 38, 41, 48, 51, 57, 60, 66, 72, 76, 79, 84 and 87 by Chris Newton

Introduction

'What's it all about, Lord?' The 'all' in the title of this book attempts to grapple with questions frequently asked by many of us who are trying to live a life of faith. The poems come as late blooms in my spiritual life. Why has it taken so long for the Lord to break through? At the age of three score years and ten, it's very late indeed! The main reason being that I have always been too busy with 'me' to listen. Better late than never!

If you are too busy with 'you', then perhaps the reflections will help the Lord to get through to you at a much earlier stage in your life.

These reflections were not just the fruit of formal prayer but would arise during everyday situations and events:

Whilst driving: Perhaps they could be a code for life's highways.

Whilst walking: Perhaps they could become a path through the wilderness of life.

Whilst dozing: Perhaps they could become a path to trod while not sleepwalking.

Whilst feeling low: And perhaps a path that leads to happiness and fulfilment.

Richard Cullen

Note: Volume 2 of 'What's Going On Lord?' is in preparation.

What's Going On, Lord?

What's going on, Lord? I asked,
How far are you prepared to go?
You spoke and asked me something,
I was shocked from the top of my head to the tip of my toes.

What's going on, Lord? You want to be one with me?
I expected You to ask that I should be one with You.
You took my breath away at that moment,
Could this really be your way, could this be really true?

So what's going on Lord?
Why would You want to be one with me?
You have turned my life's belief upon its head,
I was shaken, as You could plainly see!

Ah, how slow am I to learn Lord,
For You have often taught me and l should have seen
You made me from out of Your Eternal love,
So that You could come and dwell in me unseen.

Now I know what's going on Lord,
You have always taken the first step,
But my own love is so limited,
I failed to see Your love for me, a poor wretch.

Thank you for wanting to be one with me,
Please give me the grace never to forget,
To know Your ways more clearly,
Come, be one with me, most glorious and loving Guest.

July 2018

Turn to the Lord

When we sit in the presence of the Lord,
When we weep or when we are hurt,
When the clouds gather and are getting dark,
We may empty our minds and open up our hearts.

When we experience the power of hatred,
When Satan is in our park,
When we feel like giving up and are falling apart
We may empty our minds and open up our hearts.

When joy dies within and we struggle without,
When despair plays much the larger part,
When the good within us departs
We may empty our minds and open up our hearts.

Our minds and hearts were created
To communicate, love and not to grow apart
And the Lord in His Love and mercy,
Is always ready to help us make a new start.

So when negativity, evil or distress
Is leading us astray and up the garden path,
When we are desperate or lonely,
Let Him fill our empty minds and gladden our open hearts.

August 2018

Unlock Your Heart

When someone loses a loved one,
When their heart is full of hurt and pain,
There is a chance that the one we are mourning
Is locked out and can't reach us again.

Remember, death is only a passing
From this life to another domain,
Death was never intended to be an 'end'
But a change in the love that remains.

For love is not just human, you see,
It's eternal and even in death lives on,
Yet our bitterness, anger and pain
Can be a stumbling block for them to move on.

There is no simple answer to why a loved one has gone,
No one can reach out and touch your pain,
But your depression and anger can lock them out;
Let it all go and you can lock them back in again.

Your heart is the key to unlock the here and now,
And it can unlock the mysteries that confound
Turn the key and release your misery and pain
And your loved one will live on in your heart again.

August 2018

Melt Into Your Presence

Let me melt into Your Presence,
While in this world of sight and sound
Let me melt into Your Presence,
For there is nowhere else my soul would rather be found.

Let me melt into Your Presence,
Into Your heart so full of love,
Let me melt into Your Presence,
Here, now at this moment, let me enter O Eternal Love.

Let me melt into Your presence,
In no other encounter would I rather be,
Let me melt into Your Presence,
Your gentle Love pouring in and over me.

Let me melt into Your Presence,
O such bliss and harmony,
Let me melt into you Presence,
Forever one we will always be.

Let me melt into Your Presence,
Let us be one again as we were before I was born,
Let me melt into Your Presence,
As in that swirling, dazzling eternity of dawns.

September 2018

True Friendships

The light fades, colours fade,
Time fades, memories fade,
Courage fades, intentions fade,
But true friendships never fade.

The weather changes, the seasons change,
Attitudes change, our focus changes,
Fashions change, bank balances change,
But true friendships never change.

True friendships are like gold,
They survive testing by fire,
True friendships are like old cloaks,
They give comfort and inspire.

True friendships are like a rock,
Their foundations are sure and firm,
True friendships are as secure as an anchor,
When life's problems take bad turns.

God gives us true friends,
Not just to hold out a helping hand
But to nourish and develop a bond
That is unspoken and says, 'I understand'.

September 2018

Loneliness

Loneliness can come as a thief in the night,
It can rob us of the memories which are our birthright,
It can tear at our hearts and leave us all wiped out,
It can take away all our joy and leave us with so much doubt.

The answer to loneliness is not simple, there's a long road ahead,
It affects both body and soul and can fill us with dread
The make-up of the body involves DNA, neurons and nerves,
And a mixture of organs all working to serve.

The soul is infused throughout our body parts
Until they run out of steam and the soul departs
When a demise happens to a loved one or a friend,
The loss of our anchor leaves us alone, unable to fend.

When loneliness arrives there are no greetings or sense of fun
It descends like darkness on the bereaved and suffering ones
Silence and emptiness are all that loneliness begets,
And it rubs salt into our wounds, should we have any regrets.

But there is a physician of a high pedigree,
For He knows how we tick, for He made us you see,
In fact He never suffers from loneliness,
For in His oneness He is in fact three.

All our DNA, molecules and sinews they made,
Added a soul in their image so there can be contact always,
So tune in, turn on and listen carefully,
For they will come into our loneliness, Father, Son and Holy
Spirit, yes all three.

They made us and adore us, strange as that may sound,
For they want us to know they can be easily found,
In fact they may even fight, jostle and compete
To give us that company which we so desperately seek.

October 2018

Depression

Depression takes the heart, the mind and soul as well,
It takes them to a place within that can be a living hell
Many wear masks to disguise their mental state,
The more serious are locked in with no means of escape.

No self-esteem, no feeling good, just darkness all about,
No joy or peace, just a cry – 'please help me out!'
There is very little comfort to take the pain away,
On and on it goes, every minute, every hour, day after day.

The future outlook on life, there is little or none at all,
Then there is that tumbling feeling as if in free fall
There are moments when your centre is all over the place,
And you become convinced that there is no one on your case.

In the midst of such despair nobody can break through,
No matter what is said it doesn't seem to get through
There is a heaviness and a dullness, those terrible pair,
Followed by an aching sickness – nothing can compare.

Whilst modem therapies help in many and different ways,
There is a part which the human soul has to play
The medical and the spiritual are searching for a cure,
The one should not impede the other, that's for sure.

In Jesus there is no darkness, confusion or doubt,
He knows what the power of healing is all about
He is our creator and the greatest healer of all,
Can it really be so bad just to give him a call?

October 2018

His Greatest Story
Ever Told

There is a place within us that is exempt from all life's ills,

It is a place where only we can go, a place of peace so still

This place we call the soul, and it fires up our deepest longings,

It ignites what makes us tick and makes life's journey
without belongings.

When our lives take a turn for the worse and we are faced
with pain and loss,

When there seems no light in sight, only a heavy cross,

When our bodies are transformed and we feel a shell of
what we were,

It is then that that place within, the soul, gives our
brokenness a spur.

For the soul is not just an empty place, it was created
to be lived in,

Not an added extra to inhabit the body and lay dormant within

But a place our Creator visits and enters, there within to dwell

And is always attracted to aid us when we go through our
personal hell.

Our bodies are ever precious to Him, and like the soul
will forever last,

They are both as one to Him and are ever present, never past

And when our bodies wriggle and writhe in agony and pain,

He is suffering our torment with us – just listen and
we'll hear our name.

The long hours, the weakness and wondering how it will all end,

The fear, the feeling lost and the yearning to see our body mend,

Enter that place and talk to the One who created you,

And in the midst of it all you'll know a love and a uniqueness
that is true.

You're not just a sick person, cut off and alone,

You are the one and only, He loves you on your own,

He's not content with living only in His heaven above,

But within and all around you, feel His Presence, know His love.

Maybe these words won't move you to see Him in your soul,

To talk to the One who continues to love you and forever hold,

Or indeed even to see Him as your sickness develops
and unfolds,

But be assured – YOU are His greatest story ever told.

October 2018

What Is Eternity?

Eternity is not a place, it is in me and you,
Its presence may go unnoticed,
For some it's just taboo,
For others they protest too much, perhaps because it's true.

Why did eternity seek to come within us?
Was it to taunt or tease our minds?
Or was it because human love was earthbound;
Left to its own devices, it would not be heaven bound.

So even if Eternity is not a place,
Why did it choose to arrive in you and me?
What if Eternity is a Loving Presence,
And wishes to interact in Loving Harmony?

Now perhaps we see Eternity is not an empty void,
It is not bereft of love or joy,
Even then some are evasive and tell a lie:
'Eternity is only real when you die'.

But love cannot be held back by a lie,
Even in human love this we find,
So how can we respond to Eternal Love,
If it's not just in our minds?

For any kind of love to flourish and thrive,
At the very least it needs encounter one to one,
And the Loving Presence of Eternity is no different –
After all, Eternal Love at a distance, now that's no fun!

August 2018

Healing Love

Before I formed you in the womb,
I knew you through and through,
Such sentiments seldom thought about,
Yet they are addressed to me and you.

The great wonder of our being
Has existed before the beginning of time,
Yet even with our vast array of communications
We often use words to avoid the Divine.

In truth we all grow older with the passage of time,
Though in God's eyes we grow, never age,
He sees as one who is forever young,
Through His loving and eternal gaze.

Yes, we are all caught up in time,
But we're created by an eternal design,
So that when we are hurt in our physical bodies,
Medicine aids healing, and so does the Divine.

It is graceful to know that this God
Who brought us into time
Has always been so close to us
That He has forever called each of us 'mine'.

In our lives we use so many words,
Very few can touch us when we cry,
Yet Eternal Silence speaks louder than words,
Listen, and God will speak to us as an only child.

When we suffer, the presence of close ones is precious,
They see and hear our fear and pain,
But there is yet another who would share with you,
The Divine Creator, the One who suffered the same.

When we enter into our suffering with the Divine,
We don't have to be refined – scream and rant, He won't mind
He did so Himself in that garden and on the Cross did shout,
But through His Resurrection He brings healing about.

August 2018

Hope

Hope, hope, hope, I repeated it time after time,

But what is the meaning of hope? Is it all just a waste of time?

I don't mean 'I hope it is going to be a nice day',

But a hope that has a meaning in a deep and wonderful way.

Why hope for anything? It just comes and goes

Perhaps the 'hope' thing is just an illusion, who knows?

Yet if hope were just an illusion, what a sad world it would be,

Especially when you look into the eyes of the oppressed and
the hungry.

But then something happened, not to me but to another, a 'Son',

I stood and watched and saw Him live a life of hope, hope in
another 'One'

His hope was not for a moment, nor a year, but on and on,

He revealed His hope was in His Father, yet meant for everyone.

He hoped that all the suffering, pain and sorrow too,

Would in Him be absorbed, so allow hope and joy to ensue,

He walked in hope, He talked in hope until His hope shone
through,

But He knew that there would be a price to pay, His life, for me
and you.

He hoped that sin and sorrow which corrupted and destroyed,
Would in Him be overcome, replaced with hope and joy,
He hoped that in the life He led, His words, His deeds and truth,
And hope in His heavenly Father, that would be His proof.

He hoped that faith in His Father's will would achieve all the prophets said,
With His whole being He believed He would rise from the dead,
For He believed in the sanctity of life, with love as its central thread,
And through His suffering and death He would rise as the Living Bread.

In Christian Hope I have found my niche, here I can live, not just whine,
I can trust that Christian hope is important, enshrined in the divine,
Now I have a joy, which is the first fruit of Hope, a Joy which is really mine,
To think that when I started out, I thought Hope a waste of time!

August 2018

Christmas Night

Evil looked on with hateful eyes,
To see within the newborn Child,
This cannot be, He must not get in our way,
For so long with sin we have held sway.

No little child, no newborn within,
Can stop the mighty march of sin,
How dare He stand in place of man,
And halt the work to have all damned?

Let's rid this world of tiny limbs
And carry on the march of sin,
This tiny child is no match for us,
A newborn can so easily be crushed.

In desperation evil looked about,
Perhaps His hearing they could block out,
But came the reply, 'Nothing can block out, nothing can stay,
What to all on earth the Son of Man has to say.'

Well then, His feet must be crushed,
To stop His stride from halting us,
But, came the reply, 'These little toes and ankles tied
Will soon stand up and stamp on pride.'

Evil saw its mouth did yawn,
A chance it thought, to stifle Dawn,
But while the babe did seek but milk,
A shout was heard: 'I will not wilt!'

Its tiny eyes it sought to blind,
So holding all the earth in bind,
But His stare, whilst gazing out in awe,
Did look at evil, and cried 'The might of sin will reign no more!'

Deflated and lost, there was no way in,
This tiny Infant had made His first mark on sin
Evil has no answer to the Saviour Child within,
So let us take heart when weighed down by sin.

Take refuge in Him and just BE,
For the Saviour Child will set us free
Let evil see renewed our limbs,
That ever lead us into sin.

Our eyes, our ears our mouths as well,
Can be filled with Grace and sidestep hell
So don't stay outside, enter in,
Away from evil, away from sin.

Let evil rage, spit and shout,
And let this tiny Infant blot it out,
The more it tries, the more it will lose,
If you allow the Saviour child to dwell in you.

August 2018

Time

Time is a commodity we all feel we have plenty of,
The road ahead seems long and far,
But our perception of time can be very deceptive,
For time can die as quickly as a shooting star.

Unless we understand what time is for
We will live happily with time seen as simply 'now' and 'then',
We'll work our passage and earn our crust,
Never giving thought to the bubble going bust.

Jesus came in the fullness of time,
To show us how to interact between the human and Divine
We allow so many things and events to mark time for us,
That we rush past the Divine even as we bite the dust.

Jesus won't think any less of us if we don't give Him time,
It's just that our hearts are made by and for the divine,
The colours He made, the stars in the sky at night,
We need a way to divide time that is right.

He'll never demand that time is used solely for prayer,
He'll never demand we shouldn't enjoy life's fare,
He'll only request that we meet him sometime,
And actively share in the life and love of the Divine.

So yes, go enjoy all that life has to give,
So yes, live, laugh and enjoy life's thrills,
But in the midst of this. while all is going fine,
Just take a moment of time and BE with the Divine.

August 2018

The Transfiguration

In the Garden of Eden God loved to walk,
Among the gentle palms and lush green trees
But most of all, by far His greatest joy
Was to walk with His creation of humans in harmony.

It was His presence that made all hearts,
Turn away from themselves and gaze,
Always looking outward toward others' needs,
They were forever caught up in His sacred ways.

God and us ever to be as one in this world,
To walk, to talk, to grow and be,
A harmony of human and divine,
And with one another in everything to be at ease.

Then came sin and broke the bond,
The world ceased to be a place of harmony,
It descended into chaos, a world gone wrong,
That loving and real Presence was gone.

Now Faith would replace that original state
In which God walked about our human place
But the Prophets a proclamation did make
That God would come again and His presence reawake.

And on that day when up the mount He climbed,
His apostles in tow, He began to shine,
Lifted up, His joy was so great,
His real Presence again celebrated in this earthly place.

August 2018

Presence Through Quietness

What was it that I ran from?
What was it that kept You at bay?
What was it in my heart and soul that I could not face?
What in me didn't want to listen to what you'd say?

Was it the silence that I feared?
Was it that I preferred noise to keep You out?
Was it because in silence I would be faced with truth?
Was it because in silence Your Love would break through?

Or was it the stillness that really troubled me,
That stillness that I must never enter above all?
Was it You in stillness who tried to enter,
That stillness I blocked, leading to many a fall?

Now I know it was neither of them,
It was quietness I ran from all along,
For silence and stillness are just handmaids, you see,
It was in quietness that I heard Your love songs.

All along You were leading me to quietness,
Through silence and stillness I found rest,
But in quietness I entered Your Presence,
I will be forever in Your loving debt.

August 2018

The Ego

It doesn't matter who any of us are,
No matter what position or standing we hold,
We are governed by an ego, a self, an 'I'
That demands servitude in selfishness and suffering untold.

In lives such as yours and mine,
It's mainly 'I' first and not the Divine,
Our souls are hoodwinked by this me and 'I'
To live for ourselves, and for others never die.

'I' have my rights and no one should deny,
'I' serve myself, no one else should ask why,
My thoughts of others and their plight:
'You're on your own mate, you fight your own fight.'

Lest we forget, no false ego or 'I' had He,
Jesus never backed away from suffering and death for you and me,
His 'I' was replaced by the Father's will,
He willingly accepted on our behalf that Him they would kill.

Why would anyone writhe in pain for you and me?
Why would He sweat blood at the terror He did see?
In Gethsemane He encountered the egos of all time,
Before His cross and Calvary's climb.

Yet on that earth where He lay surrounded by all our 'I's
Darkness sought to enter His light and add to his suffering and
pain,
It hoped to achieve for all of us the perfect storm of agony,
And in that moment to achieve victory before He hung on the tree.

The darkness of all our 'I's failed in their bid to avoid the tree,
Nevertheless there was great joy, for they truly believed
That the very last words to come from our Saviour's lips
Were, 'Father, why have you abandoned Me?'

But these words were from a psalm of hope that day,
Defeat by darkness could not have been further away
And while the forces of our egos raged at the sky,
Jesus breathed His last, though in no lasting death had He died.

Only the Risen Jesus can lift the veil of our 'I's within,
Only our Redeemer can lift us out of our egos' sin.

August 2018

The Cell (Before the Crucifixion)

Whenever you feel alone in a dark and lonely place,
Pop into that cell, just go, enter that place,
There is someone waiting for you, He's never really left,
Come, sit with Him, look on His face, Jesus, this loving guest.

It's a place as dark as yours but lit by His Love,
He'll speak to the darkness that plagues you, as it does,
He'll give you all the time and space that you seek,
Never rushing you, He'll wait until you speak.

Don't be afraid because you are in the presence of God,
He created you from nothing, not from some mist or fog,
He knows your very essence, the good and bad in you,
He knows what makes you tick, and he knows your darkness too.

The first thing you will see is His knowing look,
There is nothing He doesn't know, to Him you're an open book,
There is nothing you can hide or put to one side,
Just place before Him your lonely pain, and say how hard you've tried.

Now you are in His Presence as you were before your birth,
Now you are that child again before you were sent to earth,
Now He will see before Him a holy and wholesome one,
Now He will show you how special you have become.

All your loneliness and pain attracted Him to you,

He came the moment you left your peace and light,

For He has been in that same place too,

You didn't need to come to His cell, it was always in you.

Why, Jesus?

Why is it, Jesus, that I don't see?
It's as if I'm only caring about my own security
I even boast, 'As long as I have enough for me.'
Why is it, Jesus, that I don't see?

Why is it, Jesus, that I don't share?
Only store up enough by which I can live,
And make sure that I have plenty, why care?
Why is it, Jesus, that I don't share?

Why is it, Jesus, that I won't help?
I think that my time should only be for me,
That my time is such a precious commodity.
Why is it, Jesus, that I won't help?

Jesus' reply:
You won't see unless you stop looking inward only
You won't give because you only listen to your own pleas
You won't share because you shut your ears to cries of need
You won't help because your selfishness has locked you in.

But let Me teach you to see through My eyes,
Let Me teach you to give so that you become the gift,
Let Me teach you to share so you become what you give,
Let Me teach you to help others that they may have lives to live

Remember, I made the heart that there will always be love,
I made your soul for your future with Me above,
I made you with longings so you would learn to strive,
I made you unique, so unique in My own inimitable style.

August 2018

The Eviction

The mystery of evil in this life here on earth
Is that there is no real mystery about it or its birth.
Its sole purpose is to engage and preoccupy us with 'no death at all',
And in every situation of our lives keep us in its thrall.

We all have one relatively short life on this earth to live,
But evil can manipulate us and its own ends instil
Evil is so adept at making us believe
That this life and all its happenings has nothing to do
with God, just me.

Evil must make us believe that its existence belongs
to the realm of myth
And indeed the cry of the sophisticated modern 'no evil,
just all this'
Indeed the subterfuge of evil has worked well,
'There is no life after death' would next be easy to sell.

And so like lemmings we walk through life heading for the cliffs,
Sooner or later when there is a life shift,
We are evicted into eternity - 'but no one told us we would
be dead' they said.
Evil claps its hands, licks its lips, you've been evicted and
believed all we said.

Our eviction notice from life having been served,

Evil laughs, 'It's no more than you deserve, we simply sold you the absurd'.

So next time we merrily empty our drinks and plates,

We must not forget to deposit a prayer for a room in the house of saints.

Let's not be caught up too much in the cares of this life,

Enjoy it by all means, for it brings with it its own trouble and strife,

Just don't be fooled by evil as it peddles its own myth,

To avoid an untimely eviction of the soul you were born with.

But life here and in Eternity was promised by He who hung on the tree,

He came to expose evil's myth, no more evictions would there be,

Through His death and resurrection, He created the key,

So pray: Please open the door to a new life with You in the Trinity.

August 2018

More, Never Less

Before I formed you in the womb l knew you through and through
I knew the colour of your hair and how you would dress,
But I would like you to know that in My love,
You will always be to Me more, never less.

Holding you in the palm of my hand before I sent you forth,
I gave you a heart bigger than the rest,
I gave you all the grace I had to give, so in My love,
You will always be to me more, never less.

And on that day when you were born,
Into my world with all the rest,
I put a message in your heart,
You will always be to Me more, never less.

I watched you grow in life into the person I meant you to be,
I watched you in sadness, sorrow and grief
But you always reached out to my grace to find rest,
You will always be to me more, never less.

You come to me in your weakness, and when you were at your best
You believe even when your senses tell you there is nothing there
You often walk in darkness with faith as your only guest,
Ah, you will always be to me more, never less.

Soon your life will be over and in My Presence you will be,
And I will show you that through it all I was close to you
I have always held you close, close to My sacred breast,
Then in My Presence you will know, you ARE always more, never less.

August 2018

Jesus to You

When you shed tears or cry the whole night through
Inside your heart is the infant you,
Insecure and lonely not knowing, which way to turn,
Love and caresses you long for and yearn.

You feel like an island with no one around,
Longing and yearning, you plead to be found,
But if you listen a moment you'll hear a true love,
Calling out, yet within, 'You're not alone,
I am with you and not above.'

I will dwell with you in your pain,
Your insecurity and fright,
Yes, I have overcome the darkness of pain,
I promise you light.

It never is easy, I found that too,
So I will hold you in the palm of my hand,
And share in your fear and pain,
As will My Father and the Holy Spirit too.

August 2018

Without You

Jesus, without You there would be nothing at all,
    There would be no eternity,
    There would be no eternal soul,
    There would be no divinity.

Jesus, without You hope would be skin deep,
    Joy superficial, nothing we could keep
    Peace would mean just the absence of war,
    Silence skin deep, noise galore.

Jesus, without You the end would be just that,
    All our searching would fall flat,
    The heart would simply beat,
    A burning desire would be just heat.

Jesus, without You the Father's love would not be known,
    Every day would be a false dawn,
    Tears would simply be liquid on our face,
    Eternity for us would have no place.

Jesus, without You the Spirit would have never come,
    No Spirit, no voice, so dumb,
    There would be no path to follow,
    Sorrow would just be sorrow.

Jesus, without You there would be no cross,
    Life would be nothing but dross
    No resurrection from the dead,
    No path to heaven to tread.

Jesus, without You no awareness of the Trinity in our lives,
    The Father and the Spirit would have remained in the sky,
    No wonder of it all,
    No hope of rising from our fall.

Jesus, without You no hope in the darkness of death,
   No comfort in the assurance of an eternal rest,
   A body without a soul.
   The whole of creation would exist without any role.

Jesus, without You no life without end...
Thank You, Amen.

August 2018

Why You Came

As she lay dying, I bathed her face
For me there could be no other place
Nothing morbid or downbeat here,
My love for her drove away all fear.

Then I thought of why You came
Could your reason be mine, the same?
Nothing morbid or downbeat for you,
Only your love wanted to bathe our souls too.

Men are drawn to love as a bee to honey,
It seems strange, it's the same with power and money,
But the latter has only this world for its context,
While the former has love in this world and the next.

Dying is for many a moment of no hope,
You, Jesus, saw our plight and showed us how to cope,
Not content simply with bathing our souls,
You died and rose so for Christian folk death no fear holds.

So my dearest love is gone now,
No more bathing or soothing tones,
Through my sorrows and all my tears,
In the hope You gave, death holds for me no more fears.

July 2018

Mary
(The Annunciation)

Silence descended when the Angel had gone,
Her womb had been prepared by God all along,
All her ambitions now put on hold,
Within her the Life of God as the prophets had foretold.

Hope descended, her ambitions now gone,
For what is ambition except self's desires, self's song?
God gives no place for self to be,
Hope clears a path where confusion used to be.

Joy descended, it must have sunk in,
First an Archangel, now the Creator of all within,
The source of all joy had entered within this maid of Nazareth,
For the Son of God had come to gather us.

Peace descended, her awareness of just who is within,
No more doubts or questions about Him,
Salvation for all is come because of the child in her womb,
For peace is the gift to all, peace even beyond the tomb.

The Good News descended and first dwelt in her womb,
Her humanity, without sin, had been chosen to bloom,
So her message to us all is this:
MAKE ROOM, MAKE ROOM, MAKE ROOM.

July 2018

Heaven Is Within You

Jesus said to me, as I sat in His presence one day,
Stop trying to rise above yourself
Stop straining at the leash
You need only prayer and faith in Me to develop your belief.

Don't try to get out or above yourself,
There is absolutely no reason for you to
All you need is to enter into yourself
And you will find Me there within you.

From the moment I came down into time
Heaven came down in me,
But a very strange thing happened, instead of meeting me within,
Mankind believed it should go out of itself to live spiritually.

To have seen Me is to have seen the Father,
Our Spirit guide makes us Three,
And we come to live as one within you,
Not just me, you see.

When I had risen from the dead,
I brought My life to live in you,
And through the grace of baptism,
You now share within the life of the Trinity; yes it's really true.

When then you come to pray,
Don't struggle to rise above to meet me,
Bé still and know that Heaven is within,
For Heaven is the Holy Trinity.

August 2018

Baptism

If all of our senses could only capture
What is happening in a soul this day,
The world in all its wonder and beauty
Would simply fade away.

All the greatest masterpieces,
All the poems, all the works of genius minds,
All the inventions and discoveries of the ages,
Would pale as the Father restores to the soul the Divine.

All the vastness and grandeur of the universe,
All the planets and the light of the stars above,
All the array of the heavens and its splendour,
Could not match Jesus' imprint of His love,

All the magnificence of this world's sunrises,
All the sunsets with their breathtaking hues,
All the mountains of majestic beauty,
Could not match the Spirit's grace poured into you.

All the spiritual wonders from Eden to the end of time,
All the mystics and saints and all who entreat the divine,
All the religious and the sacred priestly array,
Could not produce the embrace of the Trinity this sacred day.

July 2018

Dying Before Death

A light filled my soul the other night,
So bright I winced at the sight,
At the centre was a beating heart,
Both so full of love it hurt, I yearned for them to depart.

Then a voice spoke: 'It's only Me.'
'Who?' I asked. 'The One who died for you upon the tree
My heart that day filled all with sound and sight,
Yet very few heard or noticed My plight.'

'But why heart and light?' I asked,
'What are You trying to say to me?'
'Ah' He said, 'I see your ego is still strong.
You need my light and love to unbind you, set you free.

'Your ego has trained you from your earliest days,
It does not like My interference in any way,
But you have asked to die before your death,
I have chosen, My light and love will fulfil your request.'

'Thank You, O Fountain of Light and Love, I invite you in,
Take my ego, let me not hide behind my sin,
Then the 'I' in me, even if it is gone at my last breath,
I now have confidence in You, I will die before my death.'

July 2018

Trinity/Priesthood

'How can we give of our laughter and joy,' asked the Trinity,
'To our beloved creation whom we love dearly?'
Then a chuckle was heard as they stated with glee,
'We'll make it an integral part of the priesthood, you see.

'The laughter and joy in the Oneness of the Trinity
Is higher than any mountain, deeper than the deepest sea,
But both height and depth we'll put in the souls of all
As an integral part of the priesthood, you see.'

Then the Father and Spirit looked at the Word.
'You'll be sent to forgive sin to all in the world,
And bring Our Laughter and Joy to all who be,
As an integral part of the priesthood, you see.

'But not in power and strength will you appear,
As an infant a newborn you will be,
To show the depth of our laughter and love,
As an integral part of the Priesthood, you see.

'Show those chosen as priests they are vessels,
No matter how weak or how strong they may be.
I have chosen them for priesthood, set them apart,
To bring Our laughter and joy
As an integral part of the priesthood, you see.

July 2018

God's Gaze

I caught You gazing at my soul the other day,
I pretended not to notice the look you gave
You looked so content and satisfied,
Never had I felt so much Your child, Your child, Your child.

Your gaze continued for what seemed a long time,
What could you be looking for in this soul of mine?
When I did look, Your face said it all,
For what I saw was only love, only love, only love.

Not content simply to gaze upon my soul,
You reached out to touch, to hold,
And yet I saw my soul so full of sin.
Why would you want to hold, to hold, to hold?

Then suddenly your gaze became a touch,
I felt that l couldn't cope with so much
And as You touched my soul did spin,
In an instant You covered all my sin, all my sin, all my sin.

I simply stood wrapped in love,
Your love bursting through my covered sin,
I felt faint with joy, delirious with Your love.
Never had so much Love come from within, from within, from within.

This mortal coil of mine was transformed,
No earthly equivalent could ever come close
Truly I had been taken into Your circle of love
Father, Son and Holy Ghost, Father, Son and Holy Ghost.

Now I am returned to myself, to the norm,
Greatly changed, though not in form.
You have forever opened my eyes to the wonder of You,
To Your Presence, To Your Presence, To Your Presence.

July 2018

Dying to Self

Dying to self is not achieved with a strategy
Like the effort in an Olympian game.
It can only be done by taking on the Spirit of another
Who Himself came in another's name.

There will never be a fanfare,
Or a medal for any dying to self that is achieved,
But by an inner change of heart, not of our own doing,
Brought on by the Spirit of this Other who set us all free.

There will be no public proclamation
Of this dying that has begun,
For this dying to self can only unfold
Through the Spirit of this Other One.

Neither by fasting or discipline alone can this take place,
But by an inner change to sin brought on
By the Spirit sent by the Father,
Of Jesus who died for us in the first place.

This encounter with the Spirit is the way of dying to self
An encounter with the same Spirit
Sent by the Father through Jesus,
To obtain spiritual wealth.

Just as earthly wealth and possessions change us,
So does being draped in the Spirit's grace.
Yes, that's the one and only way
Dying to self can ever take place.

June 2018

Live in the Present

We were created to live in the 'Present'
For it is there we meet our creator and grow
A God who always and only lives in the 'Present',
In this we should copy the example of Our Blessed Lord.

While we were created only to live in the 'Present',
Evil interferes both constant and mercilessly
It leads us eagerly to look to the 'Past'
And presents a' Future' that's bright and worry-free.

In reality the 'Past' is an unrivalled torturer
And evil's enticement leaves us there in our pain and misery,
For it shows us all our mistakes and problems
And we can become trapped with no 'Present' to set us free.

The 'Future', that's where we should be, says evil,
All bright lights with wealth, its trappings and no more worries.
Then in our weakness we bask in this unreality.
Yet again evil dumps us there, with no 'Present' to set us free.

Let us heed the advice of St Augustine:
'Leave the 'Past' to God's mercy,
The 'Future' to His Providence,
And the 'Present' to his Love'.

Let us live, work and bask in the Love of God's Presence
And truly grow into who we should really be.

June 2018

Silence, That Is YOU

There is silence, there is YOU.
You have always been here, always tried to get through
Now the ears of my soul have been touched and healed,
So I hear the silence that is you, just you, just you.

There is no mistaking Your presence,
It lights up the soul as do the stars at night.
It's joyous, it's beautiful, it's You,
You in Your silence, alive, breaking through.

No earthly noise can keep Your silence at bay
For Your silence cannot be drowned out in that way.
You gently break through earthly air waves of sound
To us in Your 'Word' You have come down, You have come down.

And so You have reversed our concept of You
Up in the clouds far removed,
For never were You there but in our midst,
Speaking Your silence much louder than ever could our lips.

Dear Father, Spirit and Son,
Thank You for Your silence as one.
Thank You for being in each moment of time,
And dwelling within us in Your silent shrine.

June 2018

A Merry Dance

In days when I was young and bold I did whatever pleased me
And to my shame I played a tune, a merry dance,
In which I led the Lord, or so I thought,
Pretending to be good, you see.

A merry dance is where you lead
Another with a degree of pretence,
Indeed I was quite happy sinning
As long as I could sit on the fence.

I danced to the tune of goodness,
Yet my conscience was far away
Like a child I did what I fancied
And hoped that the Lord would stay away.

As time went on, the dance sped up
And I thought I was pretending well
The faster it went, the more I sinned.
'Now then,' said my conscience, 'You're on the road to hell.

Now every dance has to have a partner
And I was too busy sinning to see mine,
Indeed it was not I who was leading a merry dance
But God in His Love, all the time.

Now the dance is different,
I am off that road to hell
Fortunately I was never a good dancer,
For my eternal soul it was just as well!

June 2018

Eternity in Time

The more we allow eternity to enter time
The more we become our true selves.
It is not very difficult to do this,
Just sit in silence and invite God with us to dwell.

Sin demands our attention all of the time,
It takes us away from silence and God like a crime
And while noise is used as its strategy
Its aim is to destroy God's image, meant to be mine.

The TV, the computer and social media
Were designed to bring us together as one,
But sin has wormed its way in,
And silence has been replaced by fun.

Eternity gives us perspective on time
It reminds us that we were made
To build relationships not only with one another
But with the God who once in a manger laid.

So bring a little eternity of silence into time
And keep the strategy and aim of sin at bay
Don't object to having a busy schedule,
For we give time to lots of silly things in many ways.

Simply remove one of those silly little things
That fill our time each day
So that we can become more as our true selves,
And in that moment of silence make God's day!

June 2018

The Spirit's Classroom

You taught me my very first words
In Your language of love
You God's Holy Spirit,
Dwelling in me teaching Your alphabet of love.

You never noticed or indeed never much cared
That I was only versed in the language of sin;
You simply broke through with sentences of love,
Bypassing my many weaknesses within.

You didn't even notice my language of the 'world',
You were too busy instilling spiritual nouns and verbs.
You taught with such gentleness of these things,
My spiritual grammar suddenly found its wings.

You looked with such joy that day I spoke
Not as a child of the Tower of Babel
But as Your child enunciating:
I am not just one of billions, I am bespoke.

Still some way to go in your language of Love,
Yet you still hover, oh heavenly dove.
Thank you so far for all you've taught me
And the language of love that you teach is for free!

June 2018

Deep Waves of Cleansing Sighs

When a soul is freed from bondage to sin
Of the severe or lesser kind, ~
There comes from our God who always tries
'Deep waves of cleansing sighs'.

'Deep', yet there is no darkness,
'Deep', yet only light can be found,
'Deep', yet there is nothing but joy,
'Deep', yet there is no noise nor sound.

'Waves', which wash over tenderly,
'Waves', which wash us clean,
'Waves', made by an Eternal Love,
'Waves', which enfold us in Love's seams.

'Cleansing', not just of physical dirt,
'Cleansing', of sins' damage and hurt,
'Cleansing', of all fear and doubt,
Cleansing of our eyes, to see what Grace is all about.

'Sighs' that say your soul is still alive,
'Sighs' that say I will always be at your side,
'Sighs' of the joy of the Godhead within,
'Sighs' that say He will always remain even in our sin.

June 2018

Come Be With Me

I tried to find excuses the other day
Not to sit with you and pray.
As if anything created could replace
The blessedness of Your Eucharistic 'Face to Face'.

Forgive the 'grown up' in me,
I wanted to be in other things, you see.
But when I sat with you in that place
The Love and Beauty I saw; nothing could replace.

Your silent nothings, Your wonderful sighs
Echoed around in my soul of sin
You called, I came,
And oh, what joy welled up within!

Your silence is not silence at all
But Your loving presence in me.
You reach out and touch the eyes of my soul
And with Your loving touch You make me see.

Grant me grace always to drift in Your love
Send upon me Your Holy Spirit who appeared as a dove
Until I can on that final day when you call
Enter your Presence and loving enthrall.

June 2018

Strength Through Weakness

I thought I had been drawn into the unknown,
An unknown that had been waiting for me.
Little did I realise that it wasn't the unknown
But a love looking to set me free.

'Before I formed you in the womb I knew you through and through.'
So then the unknown, that love, has been with me eternally.
That love which is the eternal beauty
Wanted to awaken the beauty that was already in me.

I was of the 'world' and the 'world' withheld Your beauty from me.
I was imprisoned in my drabness,
Shackled by a world that centred on me.
A dark world, a world that would not set me free.

But like the song of the lark breaking the dawn
You did announce your beauty, and no longer was I blind.
And then I saw clearly that what had been planted in me
Was your beauty, You the Eternal, You the Divine.

All this time you never once mentioned my sins,
My faults and weaknesses never held you back.
Still you came and continue to come to me in my sin
So now I have nothing left to hide from, nor love will I ever lack.

How could I ever again not trust in You?
For You live with my sin and dwell in my shame.
You call me from my unrest to live in Your rest,
For You have truly called me by name.

May 2018

Friendship

There are three things every friendship must have:
Sharing, caring and daring.
With these three qualities
Friendships will grow with love unsparing.

Sharing your likes and the way that you tick,
Sharing your hopes in the future you pick,
Sharing your lives no matter what,
Sharing each other's presence, never watching the clock.

Caring about one another in life's ups and downs,
Caring to visit even when rushing around.
Caring enough to sit and learn,
Caring enough to listen and discern.

Daring to say what an outsider would not
Daring to walk in without having to knock.
Daring to feel you can say what you like
Daring to reproach and not be told, 'On your bike!'

May 2018

The Spoken Word of Silence

I always thought that silence was the absence of noise
That is, until I heard Your voice.
Yours the 'Voice of Silence'
That wakes the soul out of its stupor in the night.

l am quite unable to explain it,
This 'Silence of Your Voice',
For your 'Word' that invites my soul
Makes my whole being rejoice.

l hear more in the 'Silence of Your Voice'
Than in all the clamour of the world,
For the 'Silence that is your Word'
Enters the soul with a love never before heard.

The emptiness that was in me
Is now filled with Your awe-ful noise,
And the emptiness that left me lost is gone.
There is now no void.

I now know the difference of the word of the world
And 'Your Word' that speaks;
The first is babble and noise all around me,
'Your spoken Word of Silence' is to the soul an eternal treat.

Saints

Saints are not those who think themselves perfect
But are always aware of their imperfections.
Saints are not sinless,
But acknowledge their sinfulness.

Saints are not those who think they are always right
But those who know when they have done wrong.
It does not mean that they have no problems in life,
But they are ready to face them when they arise.

Saints are not those who are self-reliant
But accept the need of God's Grace in each moment.
It does not mean that they are never selfish
But they accept how wrong it is to put self first.

Saints never perceive themselves as being holy
But know when they have rejected holiness.
It does not mean they have all the answers
But they know the One who has.

Saints do not measure life in terms of great moments
But see beauty even in the mundane.
It does not mean that they never fall from grace
But they seek forgiveness when they do.

2018

The Spiritual Life

Does it really matter at all
How much in the spiritual life we grow?
Whether in unitive or illuminative states,
All that really matters is that God knows.

All I really know,
Is that a living spirituality
Is not within my power,
Is not determined by me.

No amount of sitting in prayer
Will elevate me to the heights
Of a St Teresa of Avila or St John of the Cross;
This can only be achieved by the indwelling of Christ.

So I give myself this advice
As I am called to prayer:
'Don't worry when you sit yourself down
You don't have to entertain God who is there'.

I simply sit and wait in silence
Deliberately spending time
With a God who I know loves me,
And who comes close in His own time.

If God chooses to enter my life
And enlighten me from within,
It's no thanks to my own efforts
But to Him, His will, His whim.

September 2017

Little Fingers of Prayer

Sometimes the actions of a child
Can teach us more than learned books;
The secret of this learning is the Holy Spirit
Who teaches us how to look.

As I sat in church one Sunday
The words of the sermon were filling the air
In front of me was a child on his father's lap
Looking into his face, a face full of loving care.

The child reached up with his little fingers
And touched the contours of his father's face
The child's eyes full of love and trust;
A discovery was taking place.

Now and then he would sit up
And look at his father's face as if unclear,
Wrap his arms around his neck
And whisper in his ear.

'I love you daddy,' he said
The father relished the embrace,
Then the child, pulling back, looked at him again
And then gently kissed his loving face.

In this scene I saw an image of prayer revealed
For, like the child, in prayer, we are on our Father's lap
Reaching out and searching like the child with little fingers
For a faith we feel we lack.

With our little fingers of prayer
We search His loving face
To feel the contours of his love for us
And know we are in His loving grace.

Like a child with our little fingers of prayer
We search His eyes, His ears, His mouth,
And when our little fingers of prayer are all done,
We discover that trust is what it's all about.

At times we too feel unclear
And wrap our arms around his neck
Whisper gently in His ear
'I am weak in faith, please help this poor wretch.'

So never stop using your little lingers of prayer
And discover how to love
For our little fingers of prayer
Reveal God is here with us, not above.

September 2017

Who is Christmas For?

This Christmas, as with others before
Will be hijacked by commerce, that's a cert
All lights, tinsel and those oft-repeated songs
Devoid of the truth of Our Saviour's birth.

Many homes throughout the land
Will collaborate in this commercial fayre
All lights, tinsel and those oft-repeated songs
But about the birth of Christ they do not care.

Sadly many hearts and souls
Throughout this Holy Season will also be bereft
Of the real joy of Christmas
For of Christ they couldn't care less.

Yet there a faithful few
Who at the stable there
Will come like the bewildered shepherds
And stand in awe and just stare.

So for these faithful few
Who are graced as were Joseph and Mary
Know the truth of this Holy Night
And truly deck their souls with joy and be merry.

Therefore the message of this child our Saviour
Who has come to be among us
Is that His Eternal love and truth
Will live on in hearts that hunger.

December 2017

Hope Found After Suicide

(for a young person)

Treat my memory gently
Speak to my soul with peace
Forgive me with the love I know you have
And to your hearts I shall ever speak.

The life you both gave to me
Will always live on and on
The sadness that finally took me
Is now forever gone.

Your hurt and all your sadness
Please don't turn into despair
For God's everlasting mercy and love
Now holds me in His tender care.

I know I was still so young
You never did me any harm
So now reach out in faith
And share with me my calm.

Don't punish or accuse yourselves
Of any hurt to me or neglect
For your example and gift of faith
Has enabled my eternal rest.

November 2017

Resurrection Message

Words of comfort, words of joy
The 'sting of death' can never destroy
That in His rising and journeying to hell
Was His first message: ALL IS WELL.

Yet we fall and fail, but that's okay
Jesus knows where our weaknesses lay
But by rising from the dead He would say
That His risen love can guide us another way.

No darkness, only light
No wrong, only right
No worry, only peace
No stress, only release.

O Heavenly heart of love
You came down to us from above
To dwell in us that we
May know your power to set us free.

September 2017

Here In Your Pain

I hesitate to ask
About your suffering and distress
Lest you need a space
To make sense of all the mess.

I can't take on your fear
I cannot feel your pain
Yet I know your hurt and anger
As 'Why me? Why now?' you proclaim.

Just think of it in this way
Dear heart in such distress
Your sadness and your pain
Has invited a very special guest.

He's not after food
Or the usual visitors' fare
Not even a bed to sleep on
As he arrives to dwell with you there.

His one avowed intent
To simply come and stay
In the midst of your pain and suffering
To offer His curative way

No noise in the night
No demands in the day
Just to share with you each moment
Of what He brings and has to say

No one is an island
No one need be alone
For a creator's love, like a mother's
Shines love from every sinew, every bone.

Let him then hold you
In your anger and distress
No need to appear strong
With your heavenly Guest.

Suffering and pain
Was His from the start.
He has walked that lonely road
He knows well it's no walk in the park.

So you and He together
As you live in your hurt and pain
Hold hands, touch hearts, connect with another
You won't lose, only gain.

Suffering is the hardest mystery
So difficult to explain
So Jesus has brought His father
Who enabled the resurrection from pain.

So not all is lost
Though there's still a long way to go
For the spirit of them both
Has also arrived in your abode.

Don't worry about room
For love takes up no space
The Trinity of Resurrection
Will bring comfort, healing and grace.

September 2017

Let Them Go

Memories are but moments in time
Which after a death seem to persist
They are snippets of what once was
A tunnel down which we skip.

Memories of things once said or done
Plague or please
At times in equal measure
Yet they can be fickle or tease.

Their face, their smile, their look appear
Their voice, their laugh, all seem so clear.
Then we are faced with the awful truth
They are not here and will never again appear.

Solace and comfort are yours to find
If you don't let your heart become a shrine
Their existence is simply changed, not ended
For they, like us, are broken and need to be mended.

The more we will not let them go
The more unrest in ourselves we sow
Don't let them be your puppets
Cut the strings and let them go.

Let not our memories determine their fate
Let them go, for heaven's sake
That they might enter in
God's holy and blessed state.

November 2017

Thank You, Mum

When we lose a mother in death
And her body is no longer there
The umbilical cord is cut again
And we wonder how we will fare.

The infant child within us
Takes over for a little while
And we reach out for her loving hands
That cradled each cry and each smile.

The world seems emptier now
And we have to learn again
Its only her love now, not her hands
That soothe the inner pain.

When we became independent
Our assertiveness kept her at bay
Yet in her love and care, ever watchful
Her eyes spoke with love: 'It's OK.'

Now she's gone, our assertiveness
Doesn't matter a jot any more
That independence we would trade in a flash
To have her hold and soothe us as before.

Now the days of our lives are less vivid
The cares of life falter and stall
I thank the Father, Son and Holy Spirit
For their gift of the best mum of all.

November 2017

That Nowhere Place

When the road that leads to nowhere leads you to that
nowhere place,

Then search your soul for somewhere and you'll find a
place called grace

At first it will seem strange and indeed might not be to your taste,

But it's better than being nowhere, and you'll have escaped
the rat race.

At first there will be a struggle with 'ME' first and `YOUR'
desires,

As you have lived only for each moment and the attraction
of their fires

But this place called Grace is not only about you but us,
them, others,

You'll soon fit in, away from sin, and who knows what's
to discover.

But this place that is called Grace is in fact no place at all,

It's a state of living and thriving in which goodness is
always on call

Not even a state but a person, Jesus, who is its driving force,

Who leads and guides us away from self and helps us
stay on course.

That road that leads to nowhere you've travelled for far
too long,

And you have often missed your cue and insisted singing
another song,

That's because on that road to nowhere you were always wrong,

For it was always about the singer and never about the song.

The singer here is Jesus and His song is tapered to everyone,

He writes the notes and melody given by the Father to
His only Son,

So the grace that Jesus is, is the road that we should be on,

And our lives should be lived for others as a witness to
God's Holy One.

It's a simple enough equation, as simple as one and
one make two,

Stop walking that road to nowhere and Grace, Jesus,
will dwell in you.

Say goodbye to selfishness and hello to goodness and truth,

And farewell to that nowhere place, and hello to a
Grace-filled you.

November 2018

BV - #0166 - 220426 - C0 - 203/127/6 - PB - 9781861519207 - Matt Lamination